LIFE IN THE SHADOW OF DEATH

Books by Michael Whitworth

The Epic of God
The Derision of Heaven
Living & Longing for the Lord
Bethlehem Road
How to Lose a Kingdom in 400 Years
The Son's Supremacy
Splinters of the Cross
Invisible Witness
Judah & the Walls of Jericho

LIFE
IN THE
SHADOW
OF
DEATH

MICHAEL WHITWORTH

ISBN 978-1-944704-69-8

Published by Start2Finish
Fort Wort, Texas 76244

Printed in the United States of America

Cover Design: Evangela Creative

In honor of my adopted dad

Jeff A. Jenkins

No one has walked with me in my grief more than you.
Now, in your own sorrow, and for your powerful, painful,
and personal demonstration of faith in grief,
I have one thing to say: I love, respect,
and am so grateful to God for you.

Also, Roll Tide.

CONTENTS

INTRODUCTION

Someone once said, "We live in a grief illiterate society." Boy, ain't that the truth. People have been dying for thousands of years, but it seems to me we aren't getting any better at dealing with it. Why aren't we? How can we?

That's what this book is about.

At the outset, I want to make something crystal clear. I am not a professional counselor or therapist. I have received no formal training in grief or grief counseling. But I did stay at a Holiday Inn Express once...

I don't have any academic credentials that qualify me to write on this subject. I won't pretend I do. This book isn't intended to be a comprehensive or even advanced discussion of the psychology of grief or death. I'll leave that to experts. No, this guide to grief is from a biblical and experiential perspective.

I was born to a set of very loving parents, and though I love my mom very much, I was always a daddy's boy. My junior year in college, Dad unexpectedly passed away in a freak electrical accident at home. As you can imagine, my family and I were devastated. Growing up, I had been around death to a decent degree—as a preacher's kid, funeral homes and cemeteries weren't unfamiliar territory. However, I had never lost anyone close to me, and certainly no one so young—Dad was just a month shy of forty-five when he died.

I remember driving home, in the rain, to be with my mom and sister—which, now that I think about it, are the ingredients for a perfect country-western song—and thinking, *No one should have to die at forty-four*. Then again, no one should have to die at thirty-four, twenty-four, or fourteen. But they do, because death is a part of life.

As I worked through the grief of losing a beloved father, I came to believe that everyone has one tough thing they have to deal with in life. Everyone. For some, it is when they are younger (e.g., childhood leukemia); for others, it's when they are middle-aged (divorce, bankruptcy); and for still others, it's when they are older (cancer). I assumed losing my dad at only nineteen was the one bad thing I'd have to face in life. Surely, there were advantages to "paying my dues" so soon; nothing else so negative would happen to me again, right?

Wrong.

Eight and a half years after Dad's death, my wife gave birth to our first child: a blue-eyed, smiley, gleeful little boy we named Daniel, after my dad. My joy knew no bounds. The kid used to sit on the floor, doing nothing but giggle. When he was little, he loved to dance, color, and read books, and he was obsessed with trains. He was a momma's boy, but I didn't mind. I love every moment I have spent with him. "Pride and joy" is an overused statement, but that's precisely what he was. To a great degree, I didn't finish grieving my dad's passing until my son's birth.

And then he died.

Suddenly.

Unexpectedly.

Inexplicably.

My son just died.

I last saw my son alive at about 11:30 pm on Monday, December 7, 2015. Less than two hours later, my wife came running into the bedroom, shouting, "Daniel's not breathing!" I bolted awake and ran to perform CPR on him while she dialed 911. The medics came quickly and tried to revive him; after about twenty minutes, they loaded him into an ambulance and took him to the local ER. I watched in the room as they attempted to revive him, but to no avail. He was pronounced dead roughly an hour after we had found him unresponsive.

To this day, we have no idea why he died a few months shy of his third birthday.

Indeed, death is a part of life. Some of us walk through its shadowy valley sooner or more often than others. But everyone dies, and everyone will deal with death if they live long enough. Moreover, everyone at some point will walk with *someone else* through the valley of death's shadow. How do we walk with them? How do we help others grieve? What can we say or do and not be insulting, but be safe? We'll talk about those things.

I also will deal with what I call "unconventional losses." It isn't just death in its familiar form that we grieve; human beings grieve loss in all its iterations, such as loss from miscarriage or suicide. Even non-lethal losses are grieved, such as divorce. What can we do to help when we or others experience these unconventional losses? I want to talk about that as well.

However, before we do, I must make two things very plain.

First, I want you to understand the cardinal rule of grief and grief recovery. The first and greatest commandment is *"Thou shalt not compare losses."* I have lost both a beloved parent and a child. The pain I felt when Dad died doesn't even register on the same scale as the pain I have experienced since my son passed.

But I have no right to compare those losses to yours, even if the *type* of loss is the same. Have you lost a parent like me? I'm so sorry. However, I don't know *exactly* how you feel, because the relationship dynamic was different, as is your emotional makeup. Obviously, I don't know what it's like to bury a spouse, and I pray I never do; it would be inappropriate for me to pretend my grief is greater than yours over losing a spouse. When all is said and done, I firmly believe death is death, grief is grief, and losing someone we love really stinks. Don't compare losses. They all hurt.

The second thing I want to make known is *"Whatever you*

feel, and whenever you feel it, is completely normal." To the discussion of grief, I bring not only my own experiences with loss, but also fifteen years of helping others deal with death. I spent twelve years ministering in various churches in Tennessee and Texas; I've spent the last three years speaking across the U.S., often on the subject of grief. More importantly, I meet many who are hurting and listen to their stories.

A common thread I've noticed in my fifteen years of experience is that many are afraid something is wrong with them if they don't feel they are grieving "properly." They will say things to themselves such as, "What's wrong with me? I should be past that by now," or "If I were really a Christian, I wouldn't feel that way." There are few universal rules when it comes to grief; however, one is we all act irrationally to some degree or another, and many of us will be mystified or confused by our own emotions. Grief changes you.

That is why, whenever I would get the call as a minister that someone had passed, I'd leave immediately to be with the family, and one of the first things I'd tell them (after expressing love and sympathy, of course) was this: *"Whatever you feel, and whenever you feel it, is completely normal."* By that, I mean there is no "normal" when it comes to grief. We all grieve differently. Dad used to say no two snowflakes are alike, and no two people grieve the same.

Finally, I want to thank you for reading this book. It may be that you have lost a loved one, you are hurting, and you want to learn more about grief. I'm so sorry for your loss and hurt, and I hope what I have to say is of some comfort. Maybe you have a friend who recently experienced a painful loss, and you want to understand their journey better, as well as equip yourself to be of greater comfort to them. Thank you for picking up this book; I hope it helps you understand life in the shadow of death a little bit better.

Wherever you find yourself in the valley of the shadow of death, let's allow God and life experiences to shine some light on the path before us.

Let us become literate in grief.

PART ONE

THE BIBLE & GRIEF

THE NATURE OF STAGES

L et's begin by exploring the five "stages" of grief. I put "stages" in quotation marks because I'm not too fond of that word. I prefer to think of these stages as emotions. "Stages" conveys the idea that these are sequential, and when it comes to grief, they decidedly are not. A grieving person can go from Stage 2 to Stage 4, to 3, to 1, to 5, to 3, to 4, to 2, to 4, to 1...

You get the idea.

As I said, I prefer to think of these as emotions—five emotions we will feel as we live in the shadow of death. Virtually all of the literature on death refers to these as "stages," however, so I retain the term in this book.

Psychologists have identified five main stages of grief. We will investigate each one and observe how they are reflected in Scripture. Before we do so, however, I want to discuss three essential principles concerning the stages of grief.

These stages are what **some** *people will feel, but not* **all.** These stages are general in nature; not everyone will go through all five. One might experience only three or four. Everyone grieves differently. If you never feel the emotion of anger, or if you never find yourself bargaining, don't worry about it.

These stages have no time limit. A person might remain in one stage for a few moments while spending months or years in another. Don't place yourself on too tight a timetable when it comes to dealing with the emotions of grief. Ten years after a death, if a person is still dwelling in their anger, then that may need to be addressed. Generally speaking, however, people move through the stages of grief at a wide range of paces. If you aren't progressing as quickly as you think you should, don't worry about it. On the other hand, if you begin to feel better or "normal" sooner than you anticipated, that's OK too.

No one will experience these stages precisely like someone else. Remember, no two snowflakes are alike, and no two people are alike. No two people grieve the same way. Your experiences with the stage of denial will be different from mine. The way I go about bargaining or accepting loss will vary from your approach. That's normal. If you aren't experiencing the stages of grief like someone else has, don't worry about it.

This is why, as I said in the Introduction, I have for a long time advised people, *"Whatever you feel, and whenever you feel it, is completely normal."* So with these three points and one great truth in mind, let's explore the five stages of grief.

STAGE 1: DENIAL

The first stage or emotion of grief is denial. It is important to note that this is more of a symbolic, not actual, denial. In other words, by "denial," we do not mean a person literally refuses to acknowledge that a person has passed.

Instead, denial is often demonstrated by shock or disbelief. Denial will prompt a person to wonder to themselves, or even aloud, such things as, "Did this really happen, or was this just a bad dream?" After talking with many, many people, it seems to be quite common for a person suffering a loss to wake up in the morning and, for a split-second, think the recent death has been a horrible nightmare and nothing more. But after that split-second, the awful reality settles on their consciousness once again, and they are reminded that, yes, their loved one is still gone.

Others experience denial by expecting their loved one to "walk through the door at any moment," or that someone will soon inform them that this is one big joke, that no one has actually died. I experienced the latter when my son passed. His funeral was about two weeks before Christmas, and on Christmas Eve, I fully expected someone to knock on my front door and explain this was all a prank gone horribly wrong. My son was alive and safe, they were very sorry for the unnecessary grief they had caused, and wished me a Merry Christmas.

If only…

The stage of denial places us on auto-pilot in order for us to function in the early days of grief. Denial is God's way of allowing us to feel the emotions of grief gradually versus all at once. Were it not for the stage of denial, our initial feelings would likely overwhelm us. Thanks be to God that he has wired us in such a way that we only experience as much as our system can handle (albeit with his power, not merely our own), and no more.

I remember very well, when both my dad and my son passed away, I went into "minister mode." As people came to the funeral home to comfort my family and me, I instead acted as the one who was supposed to comfort *them*. To varying degrees, I saw my mom go into "preacher's wife mode" when Dad died, and my wife did the same with Daniel's death. I believe this was a form of denial.

One of my college professors expressed concern over how I was handling everything a few months after Dad's passing. He said, "Michael, your attitude when your dad died seemed to be, 'Well, my dad died, and he was a good man, and he's now in heaven. What's for lunch?'" I can't say he was wrong. Sometimes, denial manifests itself in an overwhelming desire not to deal with the present circumstances.

This type of denial is reflected in Scripture. In Psalm 55, David petitioned God to hear his complaint. He was being oppressed and was grieving his loss of peace. In verses 4-7, he lamented, "My heart is in anguish within me; the terrors of death have fallen upon me. Fear and trembling come upon me, and horror overwhelms me. And I say, 'Oh, that I had wings like a dove! I would fly away and be at rest; yes, I would wander far away; I would lodge in the wilderness.'"

Note that last part: David was so overwhelmed that he wanted to fly away; he wanted to escape to the country to get away from it all. How many of us, in the depths of grief, have wanted to go on a permanent vacation? This was David's attempt to deal with his problems through a form of denial. As I said previously, I believe the stage of denial is God-given. It is his way of protecting us and showing us grace in times of trouble. That means experiencing the stage of denial is completely natural; there is nothing wrong with us.

However, there comes a time when the effects of denial wear off, and we experience the next emotion, or stage, in our journey. All the feelings we have been denying begin to weigh fully on our soul or rise to the surface, and denial gives way to…

STAGE 2: ANGER

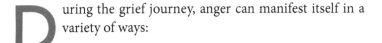uring the grief journey, anger can manifest itself in a variety of ways:

- Anger at our loved one for not taking better care of themselves.
- Anger at ourselves for not taking better care of our loved one.
- Anger at others for not doing more to prevent the death (e.g., family, doctors, drunk driver).
- Anger at God for allowing the death to happen.

It is critical to recognize that this anger is seldom reasonable or logical. Instead, *it exists in a place in your heart that reason or logic cannot access.* Do not expect the anger in your grief journey to make sense. Sometimes, we know we are angry and for no good reason, and so we get down on ourselves, thinking,

I shouldn't feel this way. But this is unhelpful. The emotion of anger during the grief journey is natural and normal. In fact, you may begin to experience the anger stage once you realize you will survive the loss you have experienced.

Scripture is honest about this stage of grief; the Bible neither makes light of it nor shames it. In the throes of bitterness, the patriarch Job spewed his invective out against the Lord:

> I cannot keep from speaking. I must express my anguish. My bitter soul must complain. Am I a sea monster or a dragon that you must place me under guard? I think, "My bed will comfort me, and sleep will ease my misery," but then you shatter me with dreams and terrify me with visions. I would rather be strangled— rather die than suffer like this. I hate my life and don't want to go on living. Oh, leave me alone for my few remaining days. What are people, that you should make so much of us, that you should think of us so often? For you examine us every morning and test us every moment. Why won't you leave me alone, at least long enough for me to swallow! If I have sinned, what have I done to you, O watcher of all humanity? Why make me your target? Am I a burden to you? Why not just forgive my sin and take away my guilt? For soon I will lie down in the dust and die. When you look for me, I will be gone.

Job 7:11-21 NLT

In the Gospel of John, Jesus received news that his friend, Lazarus, was dying. Bizarrely, Jesus intentionally delayed his departure to Bethany, Lazarus' home, instead of hastening to his friend's side to heal him. When he arrived to find that Lazarus had already passed, Martha was furious: "Lord, if you had been here, my brother would not have died" (John 11:21).

Many Christians have been taught to suppress, rather than deal with, their anger. The Bible never condemns anger per se, but rather *what we do* when we are angry (cf. Ephesians 4:26-27). During the grief journey, it is important that we feel (but not dwell on) our anger, even if it seems endless. The more we feel this anger, the more it will diminish, and we can begin to heal. Just remember that our feelings or emotions aren't an accurate barometer of anything!

As we just saw in the examples of Job and Martha, the stage of anger often most viciously manifests itself in anger towards God. But this is OK; *God is the only one completely prepared to deal with your anger*. Some Christians believe, wrongly, that we should never pour our anger out to the Lord, but that it's OK to do so to others. In fact, the opposite is true. God understands our anger when we grieve, because anger is often an indication of the intensity of our love.

STAGE 3: BARGAINING

Grief's third stage, bargaining, makes itself known in very different ways. Like denial and anger, some may experience the bargaining stage *before* a death has occurred. We plead with God, promising to do anything if he preserves the life of our loved one. King David did this as his infant son lay dying (2 Samuel 12:15-17). After a death, we may offer the same if God will preserve the lives of our remaining loved ones. We may even bargain with God to go to heaven under any circumstances; "I just want to see my loved one again."

On the other hand, bargaining may cause us, like Elijah, to beg God to take our life. In 1 Kings 19, the prophet was despondent over Jezebel's threat to his life. His panic and desperation led him into the desert where he asked to die, that he was the only servant God had left in Israel, and that he would soon die anyway at the hands of Jezebel's assassins.

Even our Lord engaged in bargaining. On the night before

his trial and crucifixion, Jesus knelt in the garden and begged his Father, "Let this cup pass from me…" (Mark 14:36). Christ knew that, by going to the cross to atone for our sins, he would be made to drink the cup of his Father's poisonous wrath. Jesus looked for any way of getting out of this assignment. But of course, he subjected himself to the will of the Father.

Bargaining's most common manifestation is in playing the "what-if" game. We've all asked ourselves these types of questions:

- What if I had been more sensitive to their needs?
- What if I had insisted they see a doctor sooner?
- What if I had sacrificed more to care for them?
- What if I had not asked them to run that errand?
- What if I had authorized that medical procedure?
- What if…

Wallowing in what-ifs is natural and normal, but seldom is it helpful. Asking what-ifs may bring temporary relief to our pain, but only temporary. What-ifs are an attempt on our part to salvage some semblance of control over the situation. Eventually, however, the reality settles in that our loved one is gone, and we can't do anything to change that. With the onset of that reality can come…

STAGE 4: DEPRESSION

Depression is very misunderstood by many people. It is popularly thought that depression is feeling sad all the time. Someone will think, "I don't feel sad *all* the time, so I don't suffer from depression." But this is a very simplistic, even wrong, way of looking at it.

Some years ago, my doctor asked me a series of questions in his attempt to discern whether I suffered from depression. He asked if I struggled to accomplish very routine, everyday tasks such as getting the mail, paying bills, or grocery shopping. The truth was that I did. He helped me understand that depression wasn't feeling sad all the time, but rather the feeling that an immense fog or cloud has settled upon you. It robs you of the strength to perform even the most routine daily activities.

More recently, my doctor and I spent several days together on vacation. As I reflected on that diagnosis more than a decade ago, he told me he had since slightly altered his approach when trying to diagnose depression. He said he would ask a patient, "Imagine your best friend (whom you haven't seen in a while) comes to town to surprise you. They call you up and invite you to meet for coffee. You love coffee, and you have nothing else planned. What would you say?" If the patient says they most likely would decline the invitation, it might be indicative they are depressed.

His illustration made sense. When it comes to college football, I'm a big fan of the Alabama Crimson Tide. Three weeks after my son died, Alabama played Michigan State in the Cotton Bowl in Arlington, Texas—just a short drive from my home. The day of the game, someone offered me a free ticket to the game, and they were great seats. I declined, preferring instead to watch the game in my living room alone. To be fair, we had had a lot of visitors in our home over the previous three weeks. I was exhausted, and the last thing I wanted was to be around more people. But turning down free tickets to see my favorite team play just a short distance from my house? Yep, that was a classic sign of depression.

Depression in the aftermath of a loss is not a sign of mental illness; we are not talking about clinical depression. Don't assume something is wrong with you if you feel depressed as a part of the grief journey. In fact, I would suggest that it would be somewhat unusual if you did *not* feel depressed to some degree. Depression is a natural and normal part of grief.

Scripture is replete with examples of depression. One of the most vivid is found in Psalm 69:

Save me, O God! For the waters have come up to my neck. I sink in deep mire, where there is no foothold; I have come into deep waters, and the flood sweeps over me. I am weary with my crying out; my throat is parched. My eyes grow dim with waiting for my God.

vv. 1-3

The image David presents is of someone trying to tread water in the ocean or the deep end of a pool, but to no avail. Wave upon wave washes in, smacking you in the face. The chlorine or salt water burns your eyes and nose. The more you struggle and fight against it, the deeper you sink. This is the effect depression can have: the more you fight it, the deeper you sink into it. Later, David adds:

Deliver me from sinking in the mire; let me be delivered from my enemies and from the deep waters. Let not the flood sweep over me, or the deep swallow me up, or the pit close its mouth over me.

vv. 14-15

David was confident God could deliver him from his hopeless situation; note David's appeal in v. 13: "At an acceptable time, O God, […] answer me." Our Lord will do the same for us. When depression afflicts us, we are never beyond God's ability to deliver and save.

The typical reaction people have to depression is to fight or struggle against it. But as we can see from David's words, this response typically causes us to sink deeper into it. Depression can seem like quicksand. That is why my therapist once suggested a different tactic for addressing depression when it comes around; it has proven helpful to me, and the strategy might work for you also.

Instead of fighting depression, I have learned to show hospitality to it. I imagine depression as a very unwelcome guest who has knocked on my door. Instead of telling it to get lost (i.e., fighting it), I invite depression into my "home" to "sit and stay a while." In literal terms, I sit in a chair and imagine depression as an embodied person in the room. I make the "visit" as awkward as possible until depression gets up and leaves because he can't take me and my awkwardness anymore! This may seem silly, but it has worked for me.

In other words, instead of fighting depression, I have learned to embrace it. I don't look for a way to escape it; I see it as a way of cleansing me. I allow depression to teach me something about myself. In my experience, if I deal with depression in a healthy way, it lifts when it has served its purpose. Depression forces us to slow down and evaluate what exactly it is that we have lost. Depression can rebuild us from the ground up by forcing us to deal with things in the great recesses of our soul that we have, foolishly, tried to bury for a long time.

STAGE 5: ACCEPTANCE

The final stage of the grief journey is acceptance. By "final," I do not mean we will never again experience the previous four stages. Acceptance does not signal the end of our sadness or grief. Rather, arriving at acceptance means we have reached an important milestone or made a significant breakthrough. Acceptance is not being OK with what has happened. Instead, it is accepting the new reality, adjusting to the "new normal."

Acceptance does not mean we no longer love the ones we lost. It means we love them more! Acceptance can bring us closer to those we have lost. After our son died, my wife had a hard time moving closer to the acceptance stage because she felt doing so meant she had not been a good mother; that she did not love our son like a mother should. Because I am a loving, supportive, and sensitive husband—I told her that was the stupidest thing I'd ever heard!

Arriving at acceptance will be a more difficult task for some than others. Particularly for those whose identity was wrapped up with the one they lost, acceptance can be a challenging level to reach. For a parent, so much of her identity was wrapped up in her child; accepting the loss of that child will thus be quite difficult. The same could be said for someone who is the primary caregiver for a terminally ill spouse or parent; once that person has passed, the surviving caregiver feels lost because so much of their life had been wrapped up in providing for the needs of their loved one who was ill.

Indeed, acceptance will look very different for different people in different situations. Sometimes, acceptance may just be experiencing more good days than bad. That's OK!

The prophet Habakkuk embodies what acceptance looks like for the Christian. Habakkuk's book begins with the prophet complaining to the Lord about the evil and wickedness around him. "Do something about this, Lord!" When God informed him of his plan to punish his people for their evil, Habakkuk was aghast. He wanted God to do something, but not that drastic! For the rest of the book, Habakkuk grapples with the terror that awaits the Israelites. At the end of the book, he confesses:

> Though the fig tree does not bud and there are no grapes on the vines, though the olive crop fails and the fields produce no food, though there are no sheep in the pen and no cattle in the stalls, yet I will rejoice in the LORD, I will be joyful in God my Savior. The Sovereign LORD is my strength; he

makes my feet like the feet of a deer, he enables me
to tread on the heights.

Habakkuk 3:17-19 NIV

Habakkuk lived in a time when agriculture wasn't just a part of the economy—it *was* the economy. The prophet, however, declared that though unmitigated disaster might come, he would rejoice in God. For the Christian, this is acceptance. It is not being OK with the loss we have experienced, but recognizing that in Christ we have a joy and peace that cannot be stripped away from us.

We will still weep in disbelief—

We will still scream in anger—

We will still bow our heads in pain—

But always with the conviction that we are not alone, for you, O Lord, are our strength.

PART TWO

MISERABLE COMFORTERS

JOB'S THREE FRIENDS

The patriarch Job might be the best-known character with the least-known story in Scripture. Sure, we are familiar with the terrible calamities that befell him in the first two chapters of the book that bears his name. We likewise know of the immense blessings God poured out upon him at the end of his suffering in the book's final chapter. We know what happens in Job 1, 2, and 42, but most people haven't the foggiest clue what lies in Job 3-41. When Job had lost everything, his three friends made the long journey to see him. For a week, they sat with Job and said nothing. I'm sure Job appreciated their presence and silence.

After seven days, however, each of Job's friends stuck his foot in his mouth.

I've always wondered who it was that first said a tacky, hurtful thing to a grieving person. Was is it in Job's day? Was it earlier? Did Abraham have to endure some inappropriate comments when Sarah died? ("Don't worry, Abe—God will provide another wife.") Was it Methuselah's widow? ("Well, he lived a good, long life.")? Around the coffin of their murdered son, did Adam and Eve cringe when that one uncouth person speculated out loud, "Clearly, those parents weren't *Abel* to raise *Cain*"!?

Chapters 3-37 of Job comprise a cycle of speeches—a discussion, if you will—between Job and his three friends. Later, a fifth person named Elihu joined in. In chapters 38-41, God finally answered Job's questions—but not really.

Take some time to read the conversation between Job, Eliphaz, Bildad, and Zophar. The primary message they kept using to beat poor Job over the head with is, "We all know that good things happen to good people, and bad things happen to bad people. You have experienced some terrible things; thus, you are a terrible person. And we will stay on your case until you repent." Consider this sampling of their statements to Job:

Eliphaz

> Stop and think! Do the innocent die? When have the upright been destroyed? My experience shows that those who plant trouble and cultivate evil will harvest the same. […] But consider the joy of those corrected by God! Do not despise the discipline of the Almighty when you sin.
>
> Job 4:7-8; 5:17 NLT

Bildad

How long will you go on like this? You sound like a blustering wind. Does God twist justice? Does the Almighty twist what is right? Your children must have sinned against him, so their punishment was well deserved.

Job 8:2-4 NLT

Zophar

God is doubtless punishing you far less than you deserve!

Job 11:6 NLT

Among the things God said when he descended in the whirlwind was this criticism of Job's three friends:

I am angry with you and your two friends, for you have not spoken accurately about me, as my servant Job has. So take seven bulls and seven rams and go to my servant Job and offer a burnt offering for yourselves. My servant Job will pray for you, and I will accept his prayer on your behalf. I will not treat you as you deserve, for you have not spoken accurately about me, as my servant Job has.

Job 42:7-8 NLT

The Lord was outraged that these three men had attempted

to co-opt or hijack the Most High to validate their worthless, empty platitudes. They would have been better off never speaking. I would like to say that you and I never act or speak like Job's three friends. I'd *like* to say that, but…

WHAT YOU *CAN'T* SAY & DO

ince the day Job's three friends opened their mouths, human beings have been saying the most insensitive things to those who are grieving.

The compulsion to say *something* to a hurting person is pretty powerful. Both cerebrally and experientially, I know it's highly unlikely I'll say anything that will make someone feel any better, but even I sometimes find the urge to say something irresistible.

In my seminars, I ask for a show of hands of all those who have found themselves waiting in line at a visitation or funeral, trying to come up with something profound to say to the family when they approach the casket. Nearly every hand goes up.

Many of us fall for the delusion that, if we think really hard, we can come up with that one comment that will make all the difference—the kind of thing that, years later, will prompt the grieving person to approach us and say, "When my loved one

LIFE IN THE SHADOW OF DEATH   44

passed years ago, you said that to me, and it made all the difference. I wouldn't have made it this far if it hadn't been for your words."

Ninety-nine percent of the time, that will never happen.

The compulsion to say *something* is powerful, but you have to fight that feeling with everything you have. In reality, there isn't much that can be said to make someone feel better, and nothing can be said to take away their pain. But, oh, how we try! When you find yourself wanting to say something comforting to a grieving friend, here is what you must *not* say:

1. Do not attempt to rationalize.

When an inexplicable passing takes place, many of us try to make sense of it for the family. To do so, we offer up ridiculous platitudes such as, "God looked out on his garden one morning, and it wasn't as beautiful as he wanted it to be. So he plucked your loved one from earth to place in his heavenly garden."

I once was speaking at a church in Alabama. In the sermon, I had talked about the loss of my son. As the worship service was concluding with a final song, a middle-aged woman made her way to the front and stood right beside me (a little too close, but I didn't say anything). I assumed she perhaps had lost a child in the past and wanted to say a quick word to me as soon as the service dismissed. Or maybe she wanted to beat the Baptists to the local Sunday lunch buffet!

Instead, she leaned over and whispered, "The Lord put it on my heart to tell you he knew something bad would hap-

pen to your little boy one day, and that is why he took his life."
Marshaling every ounce of restraint and decorum my momma taught me, I refrained from saying, "The Lord put it on my heart to tell you you're an idiot."

The reality is, no one knows why a person dies in an untimely manner. We may know the literal cause of death (e.g., car accident, heart attack, mass shooting). But we don't know what is going on behind the cosmic curtain. Some things are better left with the Lord. Resist the urge to rationalize the loss.

2. Do not attempt to compare.

Attempting to compare losses is a violation of the first and greatest commandment of grief recovery. Don't do it. I know we all mean well when we attempt this. All the same, don't do it.

It sounds too cliché to be true, but I actually overheard one widow try to comfort a friend who had just lost her husband with these words: "I know just how you feel; my dog died last week." I'm not confident the friendship survived that tacky comment.

Losing a parent is different from losing a child, and losing a spouse is different from losing a friend. For those reasons, we have no business comparing losses.

Even if we are attempting to compare the *same type* of loss (e.g., parent to parent, child to child, spouse to spouse), we must recognize that the relationship dynamics were different. Your relationship with your father wasn't the same as mine was with Dad. Have you lost a child? Yours might have been a different age or died a different way than mine. So I actually do *not* know how you feel.

Finally, it isn't just the relationship dynamics that make each loss different. It is also our respective emotional temperaments or makeups. Individuals experience grief differently.

For that reason, whenever I encounter someone who has also lost a beloved father or son as I have, I am very deliberate in telling them, "I don't know exactly how you feel, but I know enough to know that losing such a person is a terrible thing, and I'm so sorry."

3. Do not attempt to soften the blow.

When our son died, a well-meaning couple came to the funeral home and, while chatting with my wife, told her, "When you look at the moral direction this country is headed in, it's probably a good thing your son died." That explanation left us both speechless.

Another way in which almost all of us try to soften the blow is by using the tried-and-true stock phrase, "They're in a better place." I have heard from numerous individuals in my grief seminars that they found this phrase very unhelpful, and for some it was even a little hurtful. Is it a true statement? Yes. Does it help? No. Because the survivor may be thinking, "No, they are *not* in a better place. The better place would be still on earth with me." It's a somewhat irrational thought, but we think it. I personally have never been offended by the "better place" sentiment, but I can easily understand why others might be.

The impulse to downplay a loss or soften the blow is a natural one. It comes from a good place in our hearts; we see our friends in pain, and we want to try to relieve that pain. But death isn't something that can be downplayed or softened, and even if it could be, I don't think it *should* be. Death stings. Death is a tyrant. The Bible calls it "the king of terrors" (Job 18:14) for a reason.

4. Do not attempt to correct their theology.

This is a difficult thing not to do for those of us who consider ourselves the ideas police. If someone is wrong (especially on the Internet!), we feel compelled to correct them. But this is unacceptable at the funeral home. That is not the place or time. In particular, don't attempt to correct someone's theology about:

The geography of the afterlife. Whether a person's soul goes directly to heaven, hell, paradise, sheol, tartarus, or Timbuktu is, honestly, anyone's guess. I am not convinced the Bible is clear-cut on where precisely the soul goes upon death. Various verses can be marshaled to advocate multiple positions. I don't mind the debate; I mind the debate at the funeral or in the immediate aftermath of a death.

The eternal destination of the departed. Once a person has passed from this life, it is inappropriate to "preach them into hell." If a person lived a wicked life, it's usually a well-known reality to the family, and they don't need me piling on the condemnation. Instead, I want to focus on offering them comfort through my presence and actions. In addition, most of us likely were not privy to a person's final moments; they might have thrown themselves on the mercy of God and begged for forgiveness. It would not be the first time our Lord showed mercy to a sinner at the eleventh hour. In the end, a person's spiritual fate isn't up to you or me.

Why bad things happen to good people. This is an age-old question without any open-and-shut answers. It is a worthy conversation, but not at the funeral home. If a grieving family is wrestling with this question, I will not go out of my way to provide answers. Instead, it is more appropriate to affirm God's love, as well as the love of their family and friends. For nearly all of the book of Job, the patriarch wondered aloud why catastrophe had befallen him. When God finally descended in a whirlwind (Job 38-41), he never gave Job an answer.

5. Do not attempt to cheer them up.

THEIR LOVED ONE HAS DIED! Sorry, I don't mean to shout, but THEIR LOVED ONE HAS DIED! No one wants to be cheered up after that. This is akin to trying to soften the blow, but the sting of death cannot be softened.

Still, I've known some to attempt this very thing. I know of one couple whose first child was stillborn. As you can imagine, they were devastated. When well-meaning friends came to the hospital to, in their words, "cheer you up," the grieving couple was stunned. The cheer-up mission was perceived as quite insensitive, and the jokes they told weren't even funny.

Something similar happened to my wife and me after our

son died. A couple and their three children insisted on coming over to the house about a week later to do some chores and in general "cheer us up." The problem was that we barely knew them; I knew the husband a little, and the rest of the family not at all. But they imposed themselves upon us for a few hours. They meant well; most everyone does. But neither Sara nor I were in the mood to be cheered up.

6. Do not expect them to process their anger too quickly.

This has the potential to be the most alienating thing you could say or do. As we have already seen, anger by itself is not a bad thing, but what we do with it can be. Generous allowance must be given for the anger people feel in the aftermath of a loss. This anger isn't often expressed at the funeral home, usually due to denial, but rather several days after the loss.

However, there are exceptions to this, perhaps when a loved one is murdered, is killed by a drunk driver, or commits suicide. The survivors are filled with anger over how their loved one died and likely feel vengeful towards the person responsible for the death. This is natural and understandable, and we have no business expecting a person to process this anger too quickly. In general, emotional outbursts by a grieving person must be ignored and dismissed, instead of directly challenged. An exception to this, obviously, would be if someone's safety is at stake. Other than that, recognize that the person spewing this bitterness isn't their best self at the moment. If the grieving person is still wallowing in their anger and bitterness years later, that is the time for an intervention. The days immediately following a loss, however, are too soon to intervene.

Recognize that God is very forbearing and patient with us when we are awash in bitterness and anger. In 1 Kings 19, the prophet Elijah was wrestling with his own fear, anger, and bitterness. God called to him in a quiet voice, asking, "What are you doing here, Elijah?" God's patience eventually led Elijah to resume his ministry. We must learn to deal gently with people who are seething with anger when a loved one has passed.

WHAT YOU CAN SAY & DO

Enough with what a person *can't* say or do to a grieving person. What are some things we can safely say or do? I have several suggestions, but let me preface those by making one thing very clear: *Your actions and presence will always speak more—and mean more—than your words.* Too often, we overthink what we can say and undervalue simply being there for a person. When it comes to actions and presence, think critically about your relationship with the grieving person and be aware of "what you can get away with." But it is better to be bold with our actions and presence than with our words.

1. What can I safely say?

When you go to comfort someone who is grieving, whether at the hospital, their house, or the funeral home, I give you permission to say two things. If you say anything else, you deserve to be horsewhipped with a strand of spaghetti. Hard, un-cooked spaghetti.

You have my permission to tell someone:

- "I love you."
- "I'm sorry."

Anything else is likely inappropriate. There is nothing wrong with affirming your love for someone in their time of need. If you feel the compulsion to say something more, you can tell them how sorry you are that this tragedy has happened. The death of someone is always a terrible thing. Even if the person was old, full of years, and a faithful Christian, such that we have no doubt as to their eternal reward, their passing still leaves a gaping hole in the lives of their loved ones. It isn't a bad thing to express your sympathy for the pain of others.

One other thing I would avoid under certain situations is going on and on about how wonderful the deceased was and all the fond memories you have of them. Unless you know for a fact that they were beloved by their family, you run the risk of the survivor thinking something like, "A lot of people thought Daddy was a good man. So why was he a jerk to us?" Under these circumstances, it's best to stick with, "I love you" and "I'm sorry."

2. What can I safely do?

As I mentioned, your actions and presence will mean more than your words. In my grief seminars, I often ask the audience to share with me things that others did for them in the aftermath of a loss that they found meaningful. Here is a sampling:

Be present at the visitation, funeral, and/or graveside. I once interned under a preacher who was rather wise in the ways of death and funerals and loss. He gave me this advice: "When it comes to visitations, funerals, and gravesides, people may not remember if you were there. But they will certainly remember if you were *not* there." He was right, perhaps more than he knew.

When our son died, my wife and I had friends who declined to make the trip for the visitation or funeral because, in their word, "We knew you would be swamped with people, and we wouldn't get a chance to visit with you." They were close enough to us that I'd have made sure we saw them, and I wish to this day they would have come. There are still others we counted as friends whom, four years later, we have yet to hear from since our son's death, although we know they know.

In contrast, as Sara and I read the register days after the funeral, we saw on the list names of people we had never seen at either the visitation or the funeral. But their names were on the register, so we knew they had made an effort to be present, and it meant the world to us. Even more, as I walked into the church for the funeral, I saw some friends from South Carolina who had, at the last minute, flown to Texas to be present at the funeral. I was stunned. Today, I'd run through a brick wall for either of them if they asked.

When my dad died, one of my best friends took a math test at college, then got in his car and drove several hours to be by my side for several days. I'm not sure I would have made it through those initial days without him. And when Daniel died, the same friend drove six hours to Texas for the visitation and funeral out of instinct. He never called to ask if he should come. He just came. He'll never know the depths of my gratitude.

Going to whatever expense, and enduring whatever inconvenience necessary to be present—that will mean the world to the person you want to comfort. Do not underestimate the power of your presence.

Bring food, but ask first; bring it, and then leave. If the grieving person is part of a large extended family or a church, food will almost always be provided, and in large sums. In fact, I've heard from many that the amount of food brought to the house of mourning is *too* much, and I know this to be true. It's not unusual for a family to throw out a lot of good food because it spoiled before it could be eaten. But whenever a death occurs (especially in the South), the first reflex many have is "I need to take some food."

Instead, many, from experience, have recommended that you ask the family first whether they need food. For the first several days after a loss, the answer will likely be "No." Two weeks later, however, when everyone else has moved on with their lives, yet the family hasn't, the answer will likely be "Yes."

It takes about two weeks for the effects of the denial stage to begin wearing off. Up to that point, the bereaved person has been living on auto-pilot. As they start to "come back down to earth," routine things like buying groceries and preparing meals feel like impossible tasks. At the two-week mark, most people have stopped bringing food to the family, but that is precisely when the family needs others to provide it the most.

Survivors of grief also recommended that a person, when bringing food to the house of mourning, "bring it, and then leave." Bringing food is often the excuse we use to come and sit awhile with the family. We want to share in their sorrow, to have that private one-on-one time with them. In the days immediately following a loss, however, it's possible we are being an imposition by doing this. They want to be left alone with their family. Don't feel bad; loneliness will set in soon enough, and your presence will be craved when extended family have returned to their own homes and friends have moved on.

Ask if you can run errands. When a death occurs, there are often a million things of a small, but essential, nature that need to be done. Suits and dresses need to be taken to the dry cleaners. Cars need to be cleaned or detailed. When the medics loaded our son into the ambulance to go to the emergency room, Sara and I got into our car to follow, only to discover that the battery was dead. I had to jump off the car from our other vehicle (talk about stressed out!). As we left the hospital, I had to jump it off again. Someone from church later came and replaced our battery without being asked. It was a huge help.

Probably the most helpful thing someone did for us after our son's death was chauffeuring us to various appointments at the funeral home, cemetery, etc. I will not name the person who did this, for he would not want the attention. But the last thing I wanted to do at that point was fight Dallas/Fort Worth traffic at rush hour. That single act of kindness, though many would consider it a small thing, was actually a big deal to me. I could never adequately express to him the depths of my appreciation for that one act of service (among many) in our time of need.

Offer to help with various to-dos. This certainly falls under the "know what you can get away with" category. But there will be any number of tasks or chores a grieving family must tackle, and some can be completely overwhelming. Clothes and other personal items will need to be sorted and then saved, sold, donated, or thrown away. Issues related to death certificates, life insurance, cemeteries and headstones, financial accounts, closing the estate, or executing the will might require some professional assistance. Offer to help in areas in which you are competent. Don't take it personally if your help is rejected; the grieving person might change their mind weeks or months later, and the offer usually will be appreciated anyway.

Send a handwritten note, card, or letter. This is something most anyone can do, and you never know if your note will be the one the family cherishes above all others. There is nothing wrong with merely selecting a sympathy card and signing your name. But it is always more meaningful if a personal note is added. Express your love and sympathy. Share a special memory of the deceased if you have one. In fact, if there was something you *really* wanted to say at the funeral home (i.e., something appropriate), this is actually a good time to say it. Several have mentioned to me that a comment they found tacky or borderline hurtful at the funeral home would have been considered comforting a few weeks later when written in a card.

When my dad died, I received a letter in campus mail from

one of my friends and classmates. It was written on notebook paper, single-spaced, in pencil. In the letter, my friend simply talked about how much he loved and appreciated me, how sorry he was over my dad's passing, etc. I consider him a dear friend to this day, and though we don't see each other often, I remind him from time to time of that single act of kindness. I have saved and cherished that letter for fifteen years.

Make yourself available to listen. This was the one need I found to be unsatisfied when my dad passed. Many people offered to "be there for me," but when I needed someone to talk to, they suddenly had more pressing demands. Tests to study for. Homework to do. Softball games to play. Hair to wash. One college classmate, however, offered her listening ear. I accepted, and it is no exaggeration to say that the friendship that ensued between me and her family as changed my life for the better.

PART THREE

I'M HURTING, TOO

UNCONVENTIONAL LOSS

t isn't just death in its conventional form that brings us to that dark, shadowy valley. Throughout life, we grieve any number of things—what I refer to as "unconventional losses." Some of these may involve death (e.g., miscarriage, suicide); some will only *seem* like death (e.g., divorce). But one thing all these losses have in common is that many of us don't know how to grieve them properly. Some of us certainly don't know how to grieve appropriately with our friends when they go through these experiences. Life in the shadow of death is always difficult, but certain losses can make it even more complicated—

MISCARRIAGE

My wife and I have experienced two miscarriages in addition to the death of our son. While those losses were different, each one was nonetheless painful. A child died!

According to one doctor I spoke with, around fifty percent of pregnancies end in miscarriage. I thought he had misspoken, or I had misheard, when he told me that statistic. I would have found twenty-five percent to be high.

When I began conducting grief seminars, I was unprepared for the response elicited by my segment on miscarriage. Without fail, people would come forward at the end of the seminar with their own stories of miscarriage, haunted by the pain they still felt years (sometimes decades!) later and especially by memories of the hurtful things people had said to them. At one seminar, an elderly woman approached me with her story: Many years ago, she had experienced a miscarriage. When a woman at her church found out, she told her, "God knew you didn't need that child. That's why you had a miscarriage." As she related this experience to me, it was quite evident that the passing years had not mitigated the hurt caused by such a callous, cruel statement.

Miscarriage is not a new phenomenon in human history, obviously. However, miscarriage has become a greater issue of late because of an increased awareness of it. There was a time when a woman did not know a miscarriage from a heavy period, but because of advances in medical science, a woman now knows she is pregnant sooner than in the past. Thus, sadly, she knows when a miscarriage has taken place.

Our culture, however, has not caught up with science in that we do not yet know how to grieve miscarriage well. Unlike with a more conventional loss, few beat a path to your door with a casserole when miscarriage occurs. Seldom will someone get as much time off from work for miscarriage versus a conventional death. In many situations, miscarriage is treated as something less than death because the child was never born. But this is wrong! If we believe life begins at conception (and I do), and that all life is sacred (I do), then Christians are morally obligated to grieve miscarriage as they would any other loss of life, especially the loss of a child.

Recognize that grieving miscarriage can be wildly different from person to person because of many factors (e.g., how far along the woman was, the emotional temperament of those affected, whether the couple already had children). These factors do not necessarily *lessen* or intensify the grief; they just make each situation different.

What are some ways you can help a person grieving miscarriage?

- *Send a card.* Express your love and sympathy. It's likely the couple will not receive as many cards in the mail as they would with a more conventional loss. Knowing you took the time to write a brief message and mail it will mean the world to them.

- *Offer to babysit*, if the couple has other children, while they go to doctor appointments or even out on a date. In the aftermath of miscarriage, it's important for couples to reconnect emotionally, but the circumstances of life can impede this.

- *Bring food.* As with sympathy cards, it may be that not as many have thought to bring the family food in the wake of a miscarriage. But following any death, it can be a daunting task to plan meals, shop for groceries, and cook—especially if this is a task usually performed by the wife/mother.

- *Be aware of milestones, such as the due date.* Reach out to the couple and affirm your love to them on these occasions. Maybe take up a collection among mutual friends to send the couple away for a romantic weekend around the due date if that is something they might appreciate.

Finally, I want to say a special word to husbands. Do not rush your wife in grieving miscarriage. Do not expect her to "get over it" after a certain period of time. Your wife's grief over the death of this child will likely be more acute than your own, if only because she was more cognizant of the pregnancy than you were. Be as sensitive and supportive as possible.

SUICIDE

Without question, grief from suicide is unlike that from any other type of loss. When I began my research for my seminar, I discovered that grief from suicide was often referred to in the literature as "complicated grief." I thought it a bit ridiculous that experts would give it this label—*all grief is complicated*, I thought to myself. It wasn't much later, however, that I realized what they meant. Experts often liken the grief from suicide to that from murder or even terrorist attack! Not only is there a death and loss, but it is often compounded by guilt and stigma.

It is impossible to know how many suicides take place in the U.S. each year. One of the reasons exact statistics are unattainable is that different jurisdictions have different criteria for ruling a death a suicide. In California, for example, a death is not ruled a suicide unless a note is left, even though a note is left behind in only 25-30% of all cases. Officially, there are around 30,000 suicides in the U.S. annually, but experts place that number at closer to 100,000 in reality. Suicide is now the third-leading cause of death among those ages 15-25. April and May are the peak months for suicide, followed closely by the onset of the holiday season.

I have a familiar, yet uneasy, relationship with this topic. I have attempted to take my own life on two different occasions: once after my dad's death, another after my son's. Thank God I failed both times! Because of my experiences, however, I have a lot of strong opinions on the matter.

In the church, suicide has been wildly misunderstood. There are many reasons a person decides to take their own life, but if there is a common thread in every instance, it is that the person suffers from severe emotional or mental pain. In addition to this unbearable pain, the person often feels immense despair. When people choose to take their own lives, they may not be choosing death so much as escape from the torture they are experiencing.

I want to reiterate that I am not a psychologist or expert of any kind. That said, of the countless individuals throughout human history who have taken their own lives, I am certain that there were some who did so while in their right mind. Furthermore, I concede that some may have taken their lives for selfish, petty reasons (e.g., spite, revenge). But I also believe the majority of those who have committed suicide did so while not in their right mind; they suffered from some sort of mental illness. They were not fully aware of their actions, and thus I believe they do not stand condemned before God. I say this because self-preservation is one of our most primal instincts. Take an infant that is only a few months old. If that child thinks he is falling, he will panic and throw his arms out in an attempt (futile as it might be) to catch himself. When someone takes his own life, it is a violation of that primal instinct.

Let me be clear—this in no way should be taken as license for you or me to end our own lives. For all I know, if I were to commit suicide, I could have been in my right mind and have to answer to the Lord—"It is a fearful thing to fall into the hands of the living God" (Hebrews 10:31). But once suicide has happened, those left behind to grieve must take comfort in the fact that God is merciful, that he knows about whatever mental illness and/or emotional despair might have existed, and that he will judge justly. What I'm even more certain of is that we have no right to speculate on the eternal destination of the deceased—this must be left in the hands of God alone.

The notion that suicide is an automatic sentence to hell—do not pass Go, do not collect $200—is rooted in the Catechism of the Catholic church (¶2280-83). It does not have much or any basis in Scripture. Granted, there is the commandment not to murder. But it is interesting to me that Scripture merely *reports* suicide; no explicit approval or disapproval is ever given. In fact, most of those who take their own lives in the Bible later receive honorable burials with no moral comment offered. Moreover, Samson is actually remembered as a hero of faith by the author of Hebrews (11:32). The lone exception to this is Judas Iscariot, and he is condemned more for his betrayal of our Lord than for taking his own life.

If you are grieving a suicide, there are some important and unique things you need to know about the stages of grief as they relate to your situation. First, during the stage of denial, the shock of it all can be even more powerful and numbing than that of a conventional death. It is a tremendous blow, so be patient and allow yourself ample time to come to terms with what has happened. Give yourself grace.

Second, any anger you feel is natural and expected. You may be angry at the deceased for rejecting you or your family; angry at God for allowing the suicide to happen or for whatever part you perceive he had in the mental illness or emotional pain that precipitated it; or angry at others for either causing the suicide or not doing enough to prevent it. Most common is anger at yourself for what you did or didn't do. As I mentioned earlier in this book, this anger will seldom be rational or reasonable; give yourself grace.

During the bargaining stage, you might find yourself obsessing over what you could have done to prevent the suicide. You might "what if" yourself unsparingly. Remember, bargaining and "what ifs" are our way of trying to retain control of an uncontrollable situation. Bargaining helps us transition through our grief, but it can also be unhelpful. Over time, if you find yourself unable to accept the reality of loss, and instead are clinging to "what ifs," your constant bargaining could be keeping you from moving forward.

The most serious stage of grieving suicide, however, is depression. The depression caused by losing a loved one to suicide can last many months—longer than the depression brought on by a conventional death. It is around the three-month mark that many people hit rock bottom in their grief over suicide, and some begin to experience their own suicidal ideations. If this is you, I beg you to seek help from a doctor, counselor, therapist, etc. You are *not* losing your mind; you have *no* reason to feel ashamed. Rather, you have suffered a terrible emotional injury and require time, and possibly help, to recover.

When it comes to our physical bodies, we understand that various injuries range in severity. If I break my leg, that is a serious injury and needs to be treated. But a broken leg isn't as severe as a shattered knee, and while a shattered knee is bad, it doesn't rise to the seriousness of a broken hip. As we make our way up the body, a neck or back injury give special cause for concern. A head injury, however, would be considered the most serious. If you are grieving suicide, you have suffered the emotional equivalent of a terrible head injury. Give yourself grace as you heal.

One final stage of grief as it relates to suicide is one you might not expect, but it's real and natural. It's relief. Relief over suicide may seem like a terrible, insensitive thing. Yet, it is common in situations where the relationship with the deceased had become toxic or destructive, or if the deceased's condition had become so difficult that the family felt hopeless to help. If you feel some sort of relief, don't feel guilty. It doesn't mean you didn't love the deceased. It doesn't mean you are an evil person. It is a natural emotion and an understandable one.

If you know of someone who is grieving suicide, what can you do to help?

- *Do not underestimate the power of presence.* The stigma of suicide may prevent some people from reaching out or being present for the family. Make doubly sure that you show up for the visitation, funeral, and/or graveside service. Be respectful of the family's privacy, but be bold and persistent in making your concern and sympathy known.

- *Rally your church or community to support the family.* Again, because of the stigma of suicide, many will be reticent about reaching out as they normally would. Encourage demonstrations of sympathy and support.

- *Affirm repeatedly to the survivors that this is not their fault.* In my experience, those grieving suicide are almost immediately burdened by guilt over what they could have done differently to prevent the tragedy. Reinforce to them that this is not their fault, and that they did nothing to deserve it.

- *Share and solicit positive memories of the deceased.*

- *Do not speculate on the eternal destination of the deceased under any circumstances.* It isn't up to you, me, or the family. God is merciful.

- *Encourage survivors to see a counselor when they feel like they are ready.* This needs to be a decision that they make on their own when the time is right, but prompt them in this direction. Insist that they talk to *someone* who will offer an empathetic and non-judgmental ear.

DIVORCE

I once read this quote: "Divorce is as close as you get to death without actually dying." I can't personally attest to the accuracy of this statement, and I hope I never can. But all of the divorcees I've shared it with nodded their heads in agreement.

In the church, it's often said we have a tendency to shoot our wounded. I've never seen this truer than when it comes to those grieving divorce. While some churches now offer support groups for divorcees, others offer only shame to the same—regardless of why the divorce happened or who was at fault. When Dad died, my mom told me she came to realize, as a widow, that the church had not done enough to minister to the victims of divorce.

Obviously I cannot speak about the grief process on this subject from personal experience. What I have to offer is the result of research and conversations with divorcees. Nonetheless it's my hope you find something helpful in what follows.

During the stage of denial—perhaps when papers have been served—one will say things such as "He didn't really mean to do this" or "This isn't happening; she'll come back home." Others respond with projection: "*You* are the problem; not me."

If a person initiates divorce, yet knows what they are doing is wrong, they seek different ways to rationalize their decision as a part of the denial process. Still others respond with isolation—"I can't handle this; just leave me alone."

In this season of denial, remember that this emotion protects us initially. It regulates the feelings of grief so that we are not overwhelmed all at once in the beginning. Adjust your lifestyle gradually, and do not isolate yourself from your friends. Grieve at your own pace; be gracious to yourself.

Naturally, anger is quick to make its presence known in the divorce process. There are two types of anger in these situations; one is red-hot anger that lashes out: "How could you do this to me after all I've done for you?" But the second type is ice-cold anger that reveals itself through cynicism, sarcasm, and other passive-aggressive means.

If you believe your anger is starting to get the best of you, make sure you take time off regularly to cool down through prayer, reflection, or talking to a good friend. I want to encourage you to be honest about your feelings and express them to someone else. But I also want to urge you to admit that some of your expectations during the divorce process might be unreasonable or unimportant.

Bargaining while grieving divorce is similar to that of death; we play "what if," trying to sort out what we could have done differently to save our marriage. If the divorce isn't final, a person may bargain by stooping to an unhealthy level of codependency—"I'll do whatever you want; just come back. This is all my fault." I believe every reasonable effort should always be made to save a marriage, but not at the risk of putting ourselves or others in emotional or physical harm's way.

Instead of stooping to codependency, you must disabuse yourself of the notion that you are, or could have ever been, perfect. Allow friends to help you have realistic expectations. Most of all, let God lead you to a stage where you can forgive and let go.

Depression is something most every divorcee faces for a time and for obvious reasons. It's easy and natural to wallow in a pity-party in these moments—"I'll be alone forever. No one will want me after this." No one should shame you for feeling miserable; after all, something terrible has happened. Eventually, however, you will have to make the conscious and intentional decision to be better, not bitter; to live as a victor, not a victim.

Along those lines, while feeling miserable, make sure you practice self-care. Watch what you eat. Get some exercise and plenty of sleep. Also, look for opportunities to volunteer in your church or community. There is something about selfless service to others that can help lift us out of our depression.

As is true of conventional grief, the final stage of acceptance will be different for different people. One common trait, though, is accepting the finality of the divorce and embracing the freedom that comes with moving forward in life. Over time, I hope you will become a "wounded healer," someone who takes their past pain and uses it to minister to others suffering from divorce.

These are some practical things I hope will help you, but I want to stress things you can*not* do:

- ***Don't justify or intellectualize everything.*** Some things about the divorce process cannot be explained in rational terms. People do not act rationally at times. Give grace.

- ***Don't pretend to be OK when you are not.*** Be honest about your feelings. Seek a friend who will listen and support you, especially when you are not your best self.

- ***Don't replace the relationship too quickly.*** As I was reading about divorce and divorce recovery, it was striking how often experts and counselors advocated for the "two-year rule." A divorcee should allow two years to pass before they attempt to replace the relationship. Replacing it too soon could bring only more heartache. After two years, however, there is often a perspective and a degree of healing that will bless your future relationships.

How can you help someone *else* struggling with divorce?

Offer to babysit. Childcare can be challenging to arrange at times for a married couple—how much more so for single parents? Caring for their kids while they run errands, attend meetings and appointments, or have some time to themselves can be a great blessing.

Invite the divorcee over to eat—but don't do it with a bunch of other married couples! This will absolutely leave them feeling isolated. Additionally, remember holidays and make sure they have a place to celebrate.

Give them a non-judgmental, empathetic ear for their sorrows and complaints. Allow them to be at their lowest around you; provide that "safe place" for them. But never slander their ex-spouse. I can promise they will likely do that enough for the both of you!

Be physical. You would be surprised how long some divorcees have gone without any expression of affection. Of course, this physical affection needs to be appropriate and respectful and holy. You should never make a person feel uncomfortable. On the other hand, a pat on the back or a warm hug could be the first physical affection they have been shown in a long time. Even gripping a man's upper arm as you warmly shake his hand can be enough to show him affection.

Finally, *do not rush them into dating.* Honor the "two-year rule." Your friend needs time to heal from a form of living death. His or her ex will remain in the picture for a while as issues are settled. There is a need to go through the emotions of denial, anger, bargaining, and depression before the heart can open up to another in a healthy way.

PART FOUR

THE FINAL WORD

n April 2019, I toured the Museum of the Bible in Washington, DC. Before I continue, I need to say unequivocally that if you ever find yourself in our nation's capital, you must go. The museum is spectacular. As I made my way through the various exhibits, I was struck by the mountain of evidence to the enduring worth of the Scriptures. As a Christian, I believe the Bible is inspired, that it has come to us from the very mind or heart of God. But I was also reminded, as I toured the museum, of how much the Bible has meant to people throughout the ages.

One of the first exhibits focused on the Old Testament and particularly Israel's story of life with God. From there it continued through the rest of the Old and into the New Testament, along the way providing "snapshots" of what the Word of God had meant to the people of God over many centuries. The museum went on to explore the Bible's impact on world and American history, on literature, philosophy, and science.

Without question, no book has had a more significant impact on the human race than the Bible.

Whenever I reflect on death and our experiences with it throughout human history, it's pretty dark and depressing. Because the Bible so well reflects the human condition, it paints its own grim picture of death. Within the sacred page, death is variously depicted as

- "a fleeting shadow" (Job 14:2)
- "the journey of no return" (Job 16:22)
- "the king of terrors" (Job 18:14)
- a "return to the dust" (Psalm 104:29)

Arguably the Bible's most iconic (and in some ways macabre) depiction of death is as a rider astride a pale horse with Hades on his heels (Revelation 6:8). Benjamin Franklin is famous for saying there are two things certain in life: death and taxes. That quip has always reminded me of the claim Hebrews makes: "It is appointed for man to die once, and after that comes judgment" (9:27). You and I both have an appointment with death that cannot be postponed forever, and none of us are here for very long as it is. "What is your life? For you are a mist that appears for a little time and then vanishes" (James 4:14).

Death has been our enemy since Eden, when our first parents rebelled against the word of God. Like an international contagion, death has enslaved to fear everyone who has ever lived. So it is understandable that the Bible speaks so grimly of death when it is so much a part of life. Yet, the Bible does far more than offer us a grim picture—far, far more.

Throughout Scripture, there are "snapshots"—much like exhibits in a museum—offering us assurance that death is not the end. So as we wrap up this little exploration of life in the shadow of death, I'd like for you to join me on this museum tour. Think of it as a museum celebrating the promise that death will in no way have the final word over us. Get your ticket; grab a cup of coffee from the shop inside the lobby. Are you ready for the first exhibit?

The Sojourners

> By faith Isaac invoked future blessings on Jacob and Esau. By faith Jacob, when dying, blessed each of the sons of Joseph, bowing in worship over the head of his staff. By faith Joseph, at the end of his life, made mention of the exodus of the Israelites and gave directions concerning his bones.
>
> Hebrews 11:20-22

There before us in the first exhibit is Isaac, frail and blind, pronouncing a blessing on his two sons before his death. You can read about Jacob's duplicity in securing the firstborn's inheritance on your own in Genesis 27; what I want you to consider is the faith necessary for Isaac to pronounce such a blessing.

The promise he passed on to Jacob was the one Abraham had passed on to Isaac—the one given to Abraham by his God.

It was the promise of rest in a land he would show him. Most think this promise was fulfilled when Abraham arrived in Canaan, but no—he would not live to inherit that land (Acts 7:5). According to Genesis 15, such would remain for his descendants hundreds of years following Abraham's death and only after they had suffered as slaves in Egypt. The promise had been passed to Isaac, and now it passed to Jacob—

And Jacob would pass it to his twelve boys, including the two sons of Joseph. Neither Joseph (the fourth generation of the promise) nor his sons (the fifth) lived to see the promise fulfilled. But faith believes God will fulfill every one of his promises, even if it is not in our lifetime. That's why Joseph gave strict instructions not to bury him in Egypt, for that country was not his home. He belonged in Canaan, in the land promised to his fathers. Centuries later, as the nation of Israel exited Egypt, they carried with them Joseph's coffin (Exodus 13:19).

Look at this first exhibit a second time. See Isaac, frail and blind, yet still able to see into the future to when God would keep his promise. See Jacob, frail yet worshipful, able to see into the future to when God would keep his promise. See Joseph, a resident of Egypt for over nine decades, making his descendants swear they would take him home when God made good on his promise and visited his people in their affliction.

See the patriarchs, see their faith that looked beyond the grave, and recognize that our death does not mean the death of the promises of God.

The Shunammite

> [Through faith] women received back their dead by
> resurrection.
>
> Hebrews 11:35

See the woman clutching her son in this second exhibit? He was dead not three minutes ago, but now he's alive! We don't know his name or hers. But she's my favorite woman in all of Scripture. Why? Because she refused to accept the finality of death until she had received a word from the Lord. Years ago she insisted to her husband that she be allowed to build a spare bedroom for when the man of God, a prophet named Elisha, came to town. That's Elisha there in the scene with her and her son. When the prophet realized this woman's immense hospitality, he told her that she, though barren, would have a son—and the word of the Lord came to pass.

But life is unfair, and fate can be cruel; when the boy was a teenager, he collapsed in the fields while working and died. The servants brought the dying fruit of this woman's womb to her, and the son died in his mother's arms. She laid him out in the spare room built for Elisha. Instead of allowing her community's rituals of death and burial to commence, she shut the door to the room and took off in search of the man of God. She would not accept the finality of death until she had received a word from the Lord.

When she located Elisha, she insisted that he—not his servant—come and raise the boy back to life. "You promised me a son, now he's dead, and I expect you to do something about it" (cf. 2 Kings 4:8-37). This woman was pushy and insistent; some might think her rude or in denial. But the people of God are never in denial when we refuse to accept death's finality, for we believe the power of death is no match for the power of God.

And like this nameless woman of Shunem, we look forward to the day when God will speak a final word on the subject of death. What word will that be?

> For this we declare to you by a word from the Lord, that we who are alive, who are left until the coming of the Lord, will not precede those who have fallen asleep. For the Lord himself will descend from heaven with a cry of command, with the voice of an archangel, and with the sound of the trumpet of God. And the dead in Christ will rise first. Then we who are alive, who are left, will be caught up together with them in the clouds to meet the Lord in the air, and so we will always be with the Lord. Therefore encourage one another with these words.
>
> 1 Thessalonians 4:15-18

A land fairer than day does exist. It is only by faith that we can see it afar, but it is real nonetheless. It is a land devoid of death, mourning, or pain. It is a land with no cemeteries. Though we stand on the shores of Jordan homesick for that land of promise, we have been promised that our Lord will return to lead us beyond the river, to where our faith will become sight, that where he is, there we may be also (John 14:3).

The Savior

> In the days of his flesh, Jesus offered up prayers and supplications, with loud cries and tears, to him who was able to save him from death, and he was heard because of his reverence. Although he was a son, he learned obedience through what he suffered.
>
> Hebrews 5:7-8

> For we do not have a high priest who is unable to sympathize with our weaknesses, but one who in every respect has been tempted as we are, yet without sin. Let us then with confidence draw near to the throne of grace, that we may receive mercy and find grace to help in time of need.
>
> Hebrews 4:15-16

See the man alone in the garden? A full moon's light accentuates the shadows and causes the darkness to seem more threatening. See the man's bloody forehead? Though he will bleed soon from iron stakes through his hands and a spear to the side, this is blood-sweat. The man is in agony; he knows what is in store for him over the next twenty-four hours—

The most horrific death imaginable; one he doesn't deserve.

To be sure, the Savior of the world suffered mightily on the cross. In another way, however, I believe his suffering in the garden was greater. The temptation was strong to pull the plug on his Father's master plan to redeem his people from sin and death. Hear his words: "Let this cup—the cup of your terrible fury over evil and rebellion and wickedness—let this poisonous cup pass. Don't ask me to drink this. Surely there has to be another way."

But hear his other words: "Not my will, but yours be done."

Once the guards came to arrest Jesus, all that followed was fait accompli. Jesus had made up his mind. He would be utterly obedient to his Father's will. The Father would turn his face away as his wrath descended upon his obedient and perfect Son. Jesus would feel his Father's fury unjustly. In him the wrath of God would be satisfied. He would receive what you and I deserve. He would do so that death might not have the final word over us. Through his crucifixion Jesus destroyed death and the devil and delivered us from our lifelong fear of death (Hebrews 2:14-15).

But that's not all our Lord accomplished with his crucifixion. Jesus became a man, lived, and then died so that he would be qualified to serve as our intercessor before the throne of God. He lived a life of perfect obedience to the Father and thus, upon his resurrection, was exalted to God's right hand. From that position of highest honor Jesus now "always lives to make intercession for" us (Hebrews 7:25). And who could be more convincing to our heavenly Father than his unique, completely obedient Son?

Pause and ponder that a moment. When we hurt, Jesus intercedes. When we scream at heaven, Jesus intercedes. When our tears seem unceasing—when our anger seems unyielding—Jesus intercedes. That mediation is possible only because the Savior agonized in the garden. He could have pulled the plug, abandoned the ship, rewritten the script. But he didn't. He was obedient for our sake. His obedience qualifies him to intercede on our behalf.

Father, Joe is hurting. He buried his wife of forty years last week. Please give him a double portion of your blessing, the peace that can't be understood. Surround him with your glory.

Father, Anne feels so alone. She lost her only child, a beloved daughter, to a car accident many weeks ago. Send your saints to her house to make your presence known in her life.

Father, Jill's husband took his life. Build a fortress of your protection around her heart, smother her with your love, and prevent the Evil One from deceiving her for a season.

Father, Robert's wife divorced him last year. He's struggling with his anger and his confidence in life. Be merciful to him. Send him peace and encouragement. I know exactly how it feels to suffer unjustly due to the misdeeds of others.

Father, Katie lost her baby last month to miscarriage. She's convinced she'll never give birth to a child. Listen to her persistent prayers; grant to her the same gift you gave to Sarah, to Rebekah, and to Hannah.

Yes, Jesus is Lord. Jesus is King. Jesus is God. But Jesus is our big Brother (Hebrews 2:11), the Firstborn in the assembly of all the righteous (12:23). As our big Brother, he intercedes on our behalf at the Father's right hand. Again, who could be more convincing to our heavenly Father than his unique, completely obedient Son?

I hope this truth brings you peace and warmth in your darkest hour: the fact that God sees you in your pain, that he knows precisely what you are going through, and that he cares deeply for you as his child. God sees, knows, and cares because of the faithful intercession of his obedient Son. God will not still every storm; he will not neutralize every threat; he will not cause the sun to shine in every valley.

But we have a God who walks with us every step of the grief journey. As you tread the path through the valley of the shadow of death, do not be afraid. Fear no evil.

He is with us.

ACKNOWLEDGMENTS

To Patricia Bridewell, Stan Butt, Nancy Lawrence, Paul O'Rear, Mike Peters, and Lisa Wallace. Their generosity made this book possible.

To Ron & Don Williams. For their support and encouragement.

To Robert & Emily Hatfield. For boarding a plane.

To Boo & Amanda Scott. For listening.

To Philip Jenkins. For the letter.

To Jesse Robertson. For refusing to leave me alone in my pain.

To Drew Dabbs. You've been more faithful than seven brothers.

To Tim & Pam Ashley. For dropping everything and driving many miles to practice *hesed*.

To Jeff Jenkins. For everything.

To my family. For your unconditional love and support. Each anniversary marks another year of God's faithfulness.

To everyone who reads this book of half-baked thoughts. Thank you for reading. Fear no evil; He is with us.